Hummingbirds

by Rachael Barnes

BELLWETHER MEDIA • MINNEAPOLIS, MN

Blastoff! Readers are carefully developed by literacy experts to build reading stamina and move students toward fluency by combining standards-based content with developmentally appropriate text.

Level 1 provides the most support through repetition of high-frequency words, light text, predictable sentence patterns, and strong visual support.

Level 2 offers early readers a bit more challenge through varied sentences, increased text load, and text-supportive special features.

Level 3 advances early-fluent readers toward fluency through increased text load, less reliance on photos, advancing concepts, longer sentences, and more complex special features.

★ **Blastoff! Universe**

Reading Level

Grade **K**

Grades **1–3**

Grade **4**

This edition first published in 2023 by Bellwether Media, Inc.

No part of this publication may be reproduced in whole or in part without written permission of the publisher. For information regarding permission, write to Bellwether Media, Inc., Attention: Permissions Department, 6012 Blue Circle Drive, Minnetonka, MN 55343.

Library of Congress Cataloging-in-Publication Data

Names: Barnes, Rachael, author.
Title: Hummingbirds / Rachael Barnes.
Description: Minneapolis, MN : Bellwether Media, 2023. | Series: Backyard birds | Includes bibliographical references and index. | Audience: Ages 5-8 | Audience: Grades K-1 | Summary: "Developed by literacy experts for students in kindergarten through grade three, this book introduces hummingbirds to young readers through leveled text and related photos"– Provided by publisher.
Identifiers: LCCN 2022002378 (print) | LCCN 2022002379 (ebook) | ISBN 9781644876923 (library binding) | ISBN 9781648347382 (ebook)
Subjects: LCSH: Hummingbirds–Juvenile literature.
Classification: LCC QL696.A558 B37 2023 (print) | LCC QL696.A558 (ebook) | DDC 598.7/64–dc23/eng/20220125
LC record available at https://lccn.loc.gov/2022002378
LC ebook record available at https://lccn.loc.gov/2022002379

Editor: Rebecca Sabelko   Designer: Laura Sowers

Printed in the United States of America, North Mankato, MN.

Table of Contents

What Are Hummingbirds?

Hummingbirds are tiny birds.
They are the smallest birds in the world!

All in the Family

black-chinned hummingbird

Costa's hummingbird

ruby-throated hummingbird

Hummingbirds can be many bright colors. Males have shiny throat feathers.

Flower Feeders

Hummingbirds live
near flowers.
They build nests in trees.

nest

They need a lot of food. Hummingbirds eat **insects** and **nectar**.

Hummingbird Food

insects

nectar

They have long **bills** and tongues. They reach nectar deep inside flowers.

tongue

bill

Powerful Wings

Hummingbirds can fly up and down.
They can fly backward.
They can even **hover**!

Some hummingbirds **migrate**. They follow the same path every year.

Hummingbird wings and tails buzz and hum. Some hummingbirds sing.

Hummingbird Call

chee
-dit!

19

Hummingbirds carry **pollen** between flowers. These beautiful birds help plants grow!

Glossary

bills

the mouths of birds

migrate

to travel with
the seasons

hover

to stay in one place
in the air

nectar

a sweet liquid that
comes from plants

insects

small animals with
six legs and hard
outer bodies

pollen

a dust that helps make
new plant seeds

To Learn More

AT THE LIBRARY

Burleigh, Robert. *Tiny Bird: A Hummingbird's Amazing Journey*. New York, N.Y.: Henry Holt and Company, 2020.

Neuenfeldt, Elizabeth. *Goldfinches*. Minneapolis, Minn.: Bellwether Media, 2022.

Statts, Leo. *Hummingbirds*. Minneapolis, Minn.: Abdo Zoom, 2018.

ON THE WEB

FACTSURFER

Factsurfer.com gives you a safe, fun way to find more information.

1. Go to www.factsurfer.com.

2. Enter "hummingbirds" into the search box and click 🔍.

3. Select your book cover to see a list of related content.

Index

The images in this book are reproduced through the courtesy of: Keneva Photography, front cover (hummingbird), pp. 15-16; 1000 words, front cover (backyard); Mike Truchon, p. 3; Michael Clay Smith, pp. 4-5; Dennis W Donohue, p. 5 (black-chinned hummingbird); Monica Lara, p. 5 (Costa's hummingbird); Christine Glade, p. 5 (ruby-throated hummingbird); Matt Morrissette, pp. 6-7; sen yang, pp. 8-9; Jennifer Bosvert, pp. 10-11; cherryyblossom, p. 11 (insects); Sutta kokfai, p. 11 (nectar); Ian Dewar Photography, pp. 12-13; Annette Shaff, p. 13 (tongue); Gareth Bogdanoff, pp. 14-15; Chase D'animulls, pp. 18-19; Gunther Allen, pp. 20-21; AZ Outdoor Photography, p. 22 (bills); Danita Delimont, p. 22 (hover); Achkin, p. 22 (insects); Brent Barnes, p. 22 (migrate); Vixit, p. 22 (nectar); Juergen Faelchle, p. 22 (pollen); Andrej Chudy, p. 23.